I0559317

JACQUELINE PIRTLE

Teleport into your truth

praise for jacqueline

"I love Jacqueline's books. They are great for adults and kids. We all have an inner genie and Jacqueline is teaching us how to hold on to it."

— Longtime Client and Reader

"Jacqueline's books are magickal teaching kids and adults how to listen to their intuition, emotions, and feelings."

— Longtime Client and Reader

"I love that Jacqueline Pirtle has written books about intuition that encourages youngsters and adults to listen to their inner voice and be who they came to be. I also love that she encourages parents to respect and allow their children to follow their inner genie, honor their auras when making decisions, and help them realize that they possess infinite wisdom and can learn how to tap into it. This is vital to a child's growth and development, yet I've never seen children books with these subject matters before. So, for that, I give Pirtle big kudos."

— Longtime Client and Reader

Copyright © 2024 Jacqueline Pirtle
www.FreakyHealer.com

All rights reserved. No part of this book may be reproduced or transmitted in any form or by any means, electronic or mechanical, including photocopying, recording, or by any information storage and retrieval system without the written permission of the publisher, except where permitted by law.

ISBN-13: 978-1-955059-77-0

Publisher: Jacqueline Pirtle - Freaky Healer

Editor-in-chief: Zoe Pirtle

Book cover design by Kingwood Creations kingwoodcreations.com

Author photo courtesy of Lionel Madiou madious.com

I dedicate this journal to all teens of the universe.

You make the world a better place and for that I thank you from the depths of my heart.

Dear parent and caregiver,

As a holistic practitioner, energetic living expert, and emotional intelligence teacher I have written over 17 books for adults and children supporting people to live a more conscious, mindful, and happier life.

You can find out more at:
FreakyHealer Store
www.freakyhealer.com

Hope you'll take a look!

Happiest,
Jacqueline

claim it!

This journal belongs to:

_____

_____

What's your happy place?
Go there, stay there, and never leave!

Hey sharpen-up-er!

In your own words, what's it like to be you? How do you feel about yourself at this age, and do you know how powerful you really are—especially when you understand yourself and the world in real good ways?

To get you to such a fierce place, I want to introduce you to a technique I call "Energetic Profiling™."

I bet you've never heard about such a thing, since it's not much talked about, or being taught freely.

So here we go…

What is energy?

Imagine that you are energy, and that all your energy has information stored inside of it. You job is to sense that energy and translate what you sense into thoughts, then words, which creates feelings to let you know how you feel—good or bad. Good feelings signal that you live according to your true reasons of why you are here on earth, as your physical body, whereas bad feelings mean that you are not aligned with yourself fully and completely.

This journal is your roadmap to figuring out your energy and discovering yourself to create your own Energetic Profile™.

By following the wisdom ball (don't worry, I'll explain this in a second!) journey in this book you will transport straight into your truth, leading you to find out the deepest meaning of who you really are, why you are here, and what it all means to begin with.

Powerful stuff, I know!

So, self-assessing wizard, are you ready to take the leap and teleport into your own gifts to then maybe, possibly, and probably share your wisdom with other people in the world?

I sure hope you say yes, because I know that you have it in you to teach the whole universe about living a happy and fun life.

Okay then self-examining magician, let's go and search for your clues!

And remember, you are a super star!

Your biggest fan and fellow Energetic Profiler™,

Jacqueline

(All of the above counts for parents, grandparents, and caretakers of young people too!)

P.S. At the end of this journal you will find some extra pages in case you turn into a writing machine and don't have enough space for all your results and findings—or even your urges to doodle or draw.

Go fill them up and have a blast!

DAY 1

Imagine you have 30 days to get to the bottom of who you truly are, determine what you're made of and what you're all about, claim what fits for you, and see all your gifts to enrich this world —while also getting crystal clear on how you want to live your life.

No small task, but no sweat! In this quest you are a self-mastery wizard owning the legendary help of a prophesy ball made of glass and wisdom. This seer ball has the power of showing your truest self in ways your heart already knows, but can't always grasp.

So for today, and before the start of your truth-search tomorrow, describe your epic wonder ball in detailed ways. What color is it, what about the surface; is it rough or smooth, big or small (make it fit to take with you at all times,) does it spin or sit still, is it on a stand or perfectly made for your hand? Imprint your powerful globe with your vision, brain, and heart—representing you perfectly and truthfully.

_____

_____

_____

_____

_____

_____

_____

DAY 2

Oi, self-aware wizard! Your first truth quest orders you to look deeply and without fear into your truth ball. To get ready for such wisdom close your eyes, breathe, then let's go!

Write your full name - first, middle, all of them - on the line below:

_____

What's your favorite pronunciation? Say it aloud or howl if you must, to get to the bottom of your truth. How does this feel?

_____

_____

Time for your magick ball, is it ready? Squint one eye and press the other close to your power ball. Look inside, see yourself; how do you feel about your name? Any insights on what it means to you? Is it representing a color, mood, or strength? What's the supernatural aura of your name—any sorcery or such involved? What shows in your glass globe? Push for getting to know yourself fully!

_____

_____

_____

_____

_____

DAY 3

Bravo, you nailed it yesterday—no fear, only the truth!

Today and the next few days, you'll have to be super present because we'll cover the meanings of your numbers (no math involved if that's what you were thinking.) It's your birthday numbers you will be taking under the microscope, to gain strength for you to fly. Are you focused, do you have your wisdom ball? Because be ready, it has lots to tell.

Write down your full birthdate (day, month, year):

_____

Now only eye the number of your birthday, stare at it for a bit— your other numbers will get a turn over the next few days.

Then grab your mystic ball, close your eyes, and imagine looking into it like it's a portal to see how your birthday number feels to you. Do you sense a specific gift it carries? Feel free to ask your wonder ball. Does it carry happiness, luckiness, goofy-ness, creativity, or even a smartness? Go on, write down your insights:

_____

_____

_____

_____

_____

_____

DAY 4

Hey jelly bean, ready to be seen?

Today, you and your truth ball will get real close to your birth month—an invaluable part of who you really are.

So focus truth-finder, and with your glowing ball in hand write down your birth month, then look at it for a good while!

_____

Now close your eyes and take a deep breath. Look into your glass ball and ask what you need to know about your birth month. What beans does it spill—do you see your month as small or big, do you feel how powerful it is or hear it as a loud or quiet one?

Quick, don't let the info slip—write down all the wisdom coming up and through.

_____

_____

_____

_____

_____

_____

_____

_____

DAY 5

Can you handle big? Because it's time for your birth year to see the light of day and feel the grooviness it holds for you.

Clear your thoughts with a good head shake, then from that empty headspace write down your birth-year, and look at it with your sharpest eyes!

Ready to close your eyes and give your glowing ball the stage to perform? Great! Breathe deeply and with clear expectations ask for the total reveal of your birth year truth. What do you feel, see, hear—what clues are you given? Is your number a powerful one, is it light or heavy, what's the meaning? Beware the amazing insights!

Note down the invaluable news immediately after opening your eyes—keep it fresh and clear.

DAY 6

Today's party is yours, self-finding wizard, you!

Imagine today's your birthday! And in case your mind goes "no, no, it's not my birthday," take control and just go with it. Back to business; with the most wanting eyes and hungry looks you're eyeing the biggest, most coolest and mouthwatering cake you have ever seen.

Dig into the details—what type of cake is it? Spill the beans on the flavor, size, form and color. Plus, how many candles are there? How old are you? Go on, write down your real age you are today.

_____

Peek at your age like you mean it by taking your deepest belly-breath yet—pump your lungs with energy and life!

Time to call on your wisdom ball! Look deeply into it, see yourself in this round magick to find out how fun you think your age is, and what you like about it most. How do you feel? What energy does your age carry—perhaps a big, small, fun, powerful, exciting, alive, or playful vibe? Do you have a favorite color right now? And for giggles, how would your age dress if it could wear clothes?

_____

_____

_____

_____

_____

Hey self-profiler, hope you can keep this number wisdom going and find yet another truth about yourself.

Go ahead, write down the time you were born. Ask your caregivers if needed because this new set of numerals holds gold:

_____

Look at your birth hour first—squint one eye and look, then the other and look again. Really copy/paste these numbers into your brain. Then, close your eyes and imagine seeing yourself inside your wisdom ball, at the hour of your birth. How did you feel then, what personal meaning does your golden hour carry to this day?

_____

_____

_____

Next, find the clues in your birth-minute. Look at it sharply, then close your eyes. Ask your power ball: how do I feel about my minute? What does this timing mean for me?

_____

_____

_____

_____

DAY 8

Tiny, tiny, you once were! Do you remember? No worries, your wise ball will do the time-traveling for you—after all, that's why you own one.

In the next two days, but for very different reasons, you will be asked to go back into your babyhood to investigate your birth place because the "where" and seeing the light of life - your beginnings - at this special place was meant for you. That place is yours and holds immense truth about who you really are.

So time-traveler, list your special birthplace below:

_____

Now close your eyes, breathe deeply, and feel yourself as a tiny newborn baby. Then look into your power ball and imagine seeing how you felt as that tiny earthling, so new and fresh. How did it look "where" you were born—and "when" you were born at the time? Do you like your birth-place? Are you remembering something special about your birth and birthplace?

_____

_____

_____

_____

_____

_____

_____

Aha-moment: everything is energy, and so are you!

At the smallest level you are made of energy. It's your building block and your foundation. Everything you do, say, and think is energy but also when you breathe or walk you are acting as energy. Fact is that everything about you - and life - is always about energy, and your energy is always new because that's how energy behaves; always moving and changing. Simply put, you are a walking cloud of energy!

So here is a question: if you give the energy you are right now a descriptive word, how would you describe it? What word would it be?

Next, get your seer ball and step into the wisdom of your time-traveler abilities. Go way back to the day you took your first breath. Are you there? Now close your eyes, imagine looking into your wisdom ball and sense the energy of your first breath. How do you feel, taking it? Does your first breath look like anything—what color would you give it? What spellbinding power did you come into this life with—and what special energy does your first breath have? Fun fact: you still are that energy and will be your whole life.

Did you know?

You have an inner voice, also called intuition, inside your body—it's in your head, heart, stomach… it's everywhere, it's part of you, and it's invisible because it's energy.

And today your job is to check out your inner voice in your head —of course, with your eyes closed and wisdom ball in hand.

Imagine stepping into your all-knowing ball and heading straight for, and inside, your head—with the hopes of bumping into your inner voice and that it will happily chat with you. But little did you know that it can jump at you when you least expect it, are not ready, or when you're too busy to listen. Surprise, your inner head-voice is like a chameleon: sometimes little, slow, speedy, loud, or with force.

Once found, pull yourself together and ask your head-intuition: "Do you hear me?" "What do you want to tell me?" "What do I need to know about myself?"

Journal this secured knowledge as soon as you open your eyes:

_____

_____

_____

_____

_____

_____

DAY 11

Next up, your talking heart!

Learn to hear and feel the powerful vocals produced by your never resting love-engine, filled with great feelings like love, happiness, and satisfaction.

But where would you be without a baseline…? So. How big do you think your heart is, and how strong are you in experiencing love, joy, and happiness today? Would you use words such as gigantic, huge, big, medium, small?

_____

Time to soul search! Close your eyes, imagine your gazing ball has an entry portal and that you are standing - or hanging if you're brave - at the edge of that gate, about to enter in search of your heart's voice. Go on, set foot inside! Can you hear it, see it? Are you listening to what it has to say? To make things real, put your hands on your heart—feel it beating. Then ask your wisdom ball: "What and how do I feel?" "What is my heart telling me?" Next, look at your heart: is your love engine capable of humongous love, infinite happiness, and incredible fun?

_____

_____

_____

_____

_____

_____

Can you say dark and spooky? But then again, for such a brave self-examining wizard like you, that probably does not exist!

So, truth ball in hand, take the plunge and imagine yourself deep in the darkness of your belly where rumbling is the norm and your certain-knowing exists like a north-star.

To set the stage: have you ever wandered into an amusement park full of rides, clearly knowing which one is for you—like there's no option than to ride it? Or grabbed a piece of clothing with a certain color in a store filled with clothes, just because you knew - without needing to try or look in a mirror - that it was the one? Yes or no? What did that certainty feel like to you?

That's your gut intuition, your gut feeling, and to experience it close your eyes, put your hands on your belly and breathe. Then imagine standing in front of your magick sphere with delight, just to find yourself inside thinking, "what a quiet, peaceful, dark, and odd space." I dare you to ask your gut-knowing: "What do I know, what am I certain of?" "What do I need to know?" "What do I want to know?"

Self-finding wizard, your energy powers are being tested today!

Your lungs, like some sort of well-oiled oxygen machine, invite you to fill your air-tanks with every breath in, charging your air-tanks with powerful life-force—while every breath out cleanses you of gunked up emotions, making room for more life-energy.

Try it! Take the biggest breath ever with your eyes closed, hold it for a second, then with gusto let it go. Did you feel how huge your lung-tanks are, how much life they can hold? How did you feel filling up with such energy? Details please!

_____

_____

Let's get you to where it all started; your first breath! In Day 9 you already hung out with your first puff. Do you remember?

Close your eyes, pretend you are being born right now, and take your very first breath on earth. Let's go, make it count!

How does this first taste of air in your lungs make you feel? Strong, undeniable, unstoppable? Did your lung-tanks fill up immensely? And what do you think; can a deep breath now still fill you with that same life-force, just like your first breath as a baby did?

_____

_____

_____

_____

DAY 14

Truth seeking wizard, it's time to stare into the core of your "why!" Grab your ever-knowing glass bubble and head to where you are comfortable, so you can hear what you're all about.

Take a deep breath, close your eyes, and place your laser-sharp focus onto your truth ball. Then ask: What am I here to do on earth? What magick am I here to share? What is my job, besides being alive as an earthling?

_____

_____

_____

_____

_____

_____

_____

_____

_____

_____

_____

_____

DAY 15

Today's self-assessment comes with a great question:

Can you be unshakable, to find a very powerful and strong guiding feeling inside of you? One that, when following creates harmony, while going against it brings havoc? Can you guess what it is?

_____

Let's try this another way: think of something that you would give anything to do, and without it right now your life feels literally over. You like it so much you would trade your favorite things in order to do it—even consider fighting for it or against anyone standing in your path to make it happen. Have you ever experienced feelings that strong—yes or no?

_____

That force is your incredible passion! What do you feel passionate about? When does your most powerful sense of passion strike? And how do you feel when your passion is being denied?

_____

_____

_____

_____

_____

_____

Hey there know-thyself wizard! Time to figure out the purpose of things! For that you'll have to pick three favorite material things of yours... go:

1._____

2._____

3._____

Now after each thing, write what it serves you as—find the strongest purpose of that thing. Keep it short, focused on its reasons, and don't think too hard. (For example: My phone, serves as a communications tool and more.)

Now think of yourself and what heroic purpose you have living as you on this planet! What's your purpose? How are you using your purpose? Who are you helping with your purpose? And how does your purpose make you feel?

_____

_____

_____

_____

_____

_____

_____

Best talent search project ever. Are you in gifted wizard?

Find the talents of your closest loved ones; friends, family, pets. Decide on at least 2 superstars, then dig deep with the courage of a lion to find their talents. What are you coming up with, what impresses you about them?

_____

_____

Time to point that search engine in towards yourself, for your own talents to be recognized! If you need help you can also try looking at yourself through someone else's eyes. What talents impress you about yourself, but also, what do others see in you? List at least 5 of your gifts! What are they, how do they make you feel, and what are you doing with them?

_____

_____

_____

_____

_____

_____

_____

_____

What's love got to do with a soul-searching wizard like you?

You might not immediately feel that love is important for you right now, but once you feel it, it's impossible to live without.

First let's cover the different types of love before digging deeper. There's the love for loved ones, pets, and friends; for things, activities, outings, fun times; and the love for being lazy, sleeping, napping, pranking, and being silly exists too.

But, what I really want to get you hooked on is the most powerful love there is, one that no-one else but you can claim. Your love for yourself! What does your self-love feel like, how do you practice it, and do you know how much you love yourself?

_____

_____

_____

Now grab your truth finder ball, see your whole body in it and imagine scanning yourself to find where your immense love sits. Can you find it in your head, heart, belly, or traces of it in your legs, feet, arms, and hands? Consider asking your glass ball too.

_____

_____

_____

_____

DAY 19

What's up lollipop? Sweeter than sweet is what we want today because feeling your emotions can get a bit sour at times. And that is what we will investigate now; your feelings. Are you armed with a lollipop in hand—or any other sweet that works for you?

What are your strongest emotions that you like? How do they feel?

_____

_____

What are your strongest emotions you don't like or have trouble getting control of—how do they feel?

_____

_____

_____

What would be a good game plan, or strategy, for you when you feel down; so you embrace how you feel, move forward and upward again, and feel proud of yourself feeling that strong?

_____

_____

_____

_____

Wow! Your brainpower must be insane being such a wise self-profiler, owning a brilliant ball helping you to know and see into the core of who you truly are.

So let's talk about the thinking machine in your head—your brain. How do you feel about it? Are you using it proudly or keeping yourself limited by not showing your smartness all the way?

_____

_____

Time to make your seer ball work for its great reputation: imagine jumping into your magick ball, heading straight to your brain. Have a seat in your noggin and look around. What does it look like inside, what's the mood in there? Does it feel fired up and energized—or something else? What is your brain telling you?

_____

_____

_____

_____

_____

_____

_____

_____

Hey wise wizard, you probably already know that your noggin produces your thoughts—but are you also aware that your thoughts nourish your mastermind with good or bad energy, depending on how positive or negative your thoughts are? And that those thoughts directly impact how you feel since your powerful mind has a habit of taking over?

To test this: How does your mind feel when you feed it positive thoughts? You know, the ones that feel good and come from your heart. Also, what's your favorite thought of all time?

_____

_____

_____

In comparison, how does your mind feel when you feed it negative or not-good feeling thoughts?

_____

_____

_____

_____

_____

_____

_____

DAY 22

Every self-searching wizard has wishes and dreams and every magick ball pushes its owner to follow their deepest desires.

Imagine looking into your crystal sphere with awe and excitement, wonder and anticipation, while asking: "What are my deepest wishes and dreams?" and ordering: "Show me what my heart desires!" and directing: "Please make my wishes come true."

Make your wishlist, self-examining wizard, and note down all that your glass ball is sharing with you. Don't forget to feel gratitude after noting down your wishes—or a big "Thank you!" will do too .

What's your happy place, oh curious wizard? How does your own personal playground for your age look like? What brings you joy, and gets you giggling until you snort? What says "fun and crazy" for you? What are your coolest moments, who's involved, and what's the fun all about?

In case you need help, trust your wisdom ball here!

_____

_____

_____

_____

_____

_____

_____

_____

_____

_____

_____

_____

_____

DAY 24

Food is never just food, especially not for someone like you: a hard working self-profiler, using their power to get to the bottom of the deep stuff while also maintaining a wisdom ball at all times. Just think of the energy it takes to come up with all that information and to always be ready.

What is food for you—what do you like about food? What do you not like? Do you like eating, and how; slow and steady while sitting, fast and on the go, alone to not hear others eat, in company where it's loud and crazy, outside or inside, on the sofa, floor, bed, or table? Also, what foods are your favorites—how do they make you feel? Lastly, what do you think is yucky and why?

_____

_____

_____

_____

Fun fact: food is also a possibility for play (no throwing though!) and creating art. How can you play with food? Cooking class, a food game? What about art—would you decorate food with flowers, maybe paint it?

_____

_____

_____

_____

Every winner starts as a beginner!

You need your wisdom ball for this one, are you ready?

Take a deep breath and fill those air tanks, creating more life than you have ever experienced. Then, let it go and feel how you are making space for a whole lot of winner energy for what's to come.

Now close your eyes and imagine looking into your magick ball, seeing a picture of a winning situation; you being a winner, having a winner day, winning at whatever you are doing. You are a winner!

Next, feel yourself jumping into this situation by stepping into your winner you. Stay there for a whole few minutes, feel your inner you, then jot down your experience.

How do you feel, being a winner? What are you doing, what is the winning experience you are having? Are you smiling? What are you wearing? Do you feel strong and bold? Are you happy? Who is with you?

_____

_____

_____

_____

_____

_____

_____

Hey self-finding wizard, time to get into the nitty gritty with some self-fact-checks over the next few days!

Fact 1:

What should the world know about you? What do you want your friends and family to know about you? What are you proud of yourself for?

_____

_____

_____

_____

_____

_____

_____

_____

_____

_____

_____

_____

_____

Fact 2:

Imagine you can do whatever you want to do. What will that be and how do you want to do it? Where will you do your favorite thing, and what will you need to do what you want to do?

_____

_____

_____

_____

_____

_____

_____

_____

_____

_____

_____

_____

_____

_____

Fact 3:

You have a genius! What is it and what does your genius look like? Is your genius outside or inside of you? How powerful is it? How can you use it to be a kind person and to help others?

Fact 4:

Imagine you could choose your perfect life. How would you like your life to be? Where would you want to live? What does it look like?

_____

_____

_____

_____

_____

_____

_____

_____

_____

_____

_____

_____

_____

_____

_____

Fact 5:

Imagine you get to give one gift (or more) to the world, to make it better and nicer. What would that be?

_____

_____

_____

_____

_____

_____

_____

_____

_____

_____

_____

_____

_____

bonus

Because hey, you don't want your self-search for your truth to end.

So keep on profiling wizard, there's still so much to find out about yourself!

DAY 31

Find 15 words that describe you perfectly:

_____

_____

_____

_____

_____

_____

_____

_____

_____

_____

_____

_____

_____

_____

_____

DAY 32

List 15 foods that you love, love, love:

_____

_____

_____

_____

_____

_____

_____

_____

_____

_____

_____

_____

_____

_____

_____

Name 15 activities that make you happy:

_____

_____

_____

_____

_____

_____

_____

_____

_____

_____

_____

_____

_____

_____

DAY 34

Come up with 15 ways to be kind:

_____

_____

_____

_____

_____

_____

_____

_____

_____

_____

_____

_____

_____

_____

_____

_____

What makes the world a better place? Think of 15 ideas:

_____

_____

_____

_____

_____

_____

_____

_____

_____

_____

_____

_____

_____

_____

_____

extra pages

How cool is it that you don't have to sweat the small stuff—like not having enough space for all your results and findings or to resist the urge of doodling or drawing?

Just come on over here and use these extra pages for whatever itches you have to scratch, and most importantly, have fun while you're at it!

Sharpen Up

Sharpen Up

thank you!

Let's be honest here… I have a dream team!

I could not have finished this book without the help of talented, creative, and phenomenal professionals and the guidance of ALL children in my life.

From the bottom of my heart, I want to thank Zoe Pirtle for her editorial mastery; kingwoodcreations.com for their fun and polished book cover design; and madiouART.com for an amazing photo shoot.

I'd also like to extend a huge "Thank You!" to all fans of my work and books—I created this beautiful journal for ALL the young people in this universe.

Life is spectacular with kids on our side!

and last but not least

I truly hope your child - and you - enjoyed this journal as much as I loved writing it, and if so, it would be wonderful if you could take a short minute and leave a review on Amazon.com and Goodreads.com as soon as you can.

Your kind feedback helps other children and parents find my books more easily, and to be happy faster. Consider it a happy deed for the children of the world. Thank you!

To find out more about my work and books check out:

www.freakyhealer.com

Jacqueline's Amazon Author Page

about the author

Jacqueline Pirtle is an internationally-renowned Mindful Happiness expert and the bestselling author of over 16 transformational personal growth books for adults and children.

She is a thought leader in the fields of mindfulness, happiness, energy work, energetic living and businessing, wholesome healing, and the teachings of one's soul.

Jacqueline has over 28 years of experience and has helped thousands of clients all over the world to discover their own happiness and how to live a conscious and mindfully aligned life filled with health, happiness, abundance, and success.

As the owner of *FreakyHealer* she has shared her solid teachings through her bestselling books, podcasts *The Weekly Freak & The Corporate Happiness Show*, sessions, workshops, courses and programs, talks and presentations with clients worldwide. She holds international degrees in holistic health and natural living and is certified in hypnosis for PTSD and a Reiki Master.

Her highly effective healing work has been featured in print and online magazines, podcasts, radio shows, on TV, and in the documentaries *The Overly Emotional Child* by *Learning Success*, available on *Amazon Prime* and Hacking Happiness.

www.ingramcontent.com/pod-product-compliance
Lightning Source LLC
Chambersburg PA
CBHW061324120626
46546CB00007B/2662